D1524084

Bugs

by Monica Hughes

Consultant: Mitch Cronick

BEARPORT
PUBLISHING COMPANY, INC.
New York, New York

Credits

t=top, b=bottom, c=center, l=left, r=right, OFC=outside front cover
Corbis: 10, 13. FLPA: 7, 18t, 18b. Science Photo Library: 9. Superstock: 8–9, 11, 16–17.
ticktock photography: 4, 5, 6, 12, 14–15, 19.

Library of Congress Cataloging-in-Publication Data

Hughes, Monica.

Bugs / by Monica Hughes.

p. cm. — (I love reading)

Includes index.

ISBN 1-59716-149-7 (library binding) — ISBN 1-59716-175-6 (pbk.)

1. Insects — Juvenile literature. I. Title. II. Series.

QL467.2.H84 2006

595.7— dc22

2005030626

For more information, write to Bearport Publishing Company, Inc., 101 Fifth Avenue, Suite 6R, New York, New York 10003. Printed in the United States of America in North Mankato, Minnesota.

022011
012411CGC

3 4 5 6 7 8 9 10

The I Love Reading series was originally developed by Tick Tock Media.

CONTENTS

Bugs and insects

The bugs in this book are **insects**.

All insects have a body with three parts.

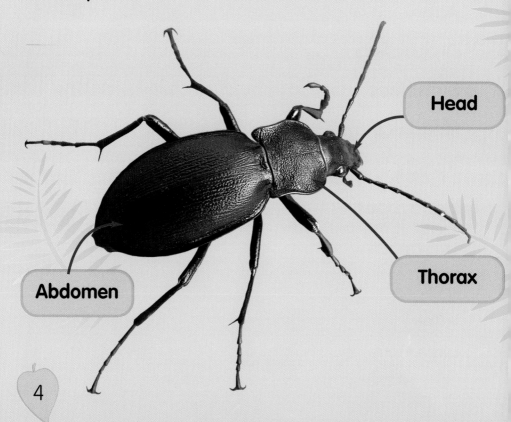

Head

Thorax

Abdomen

Most insects have two **antennae**, four wings, and six legs.

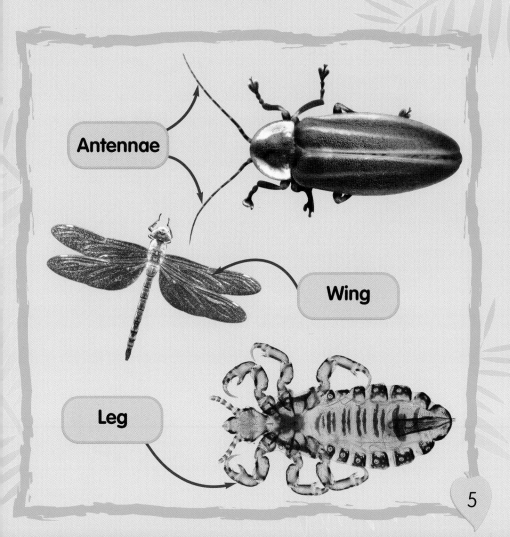

Antennae

Wing

Leg

Ladybugs

Most ladybugs are red with black spots.

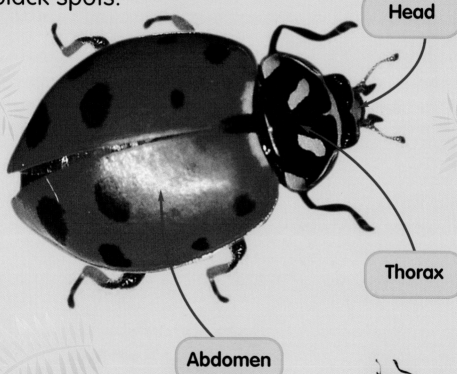

Head

Thorax

Abdomen

Some ladybugs are yellow.

Ladybugs live in gardens and parks.

They eat **aphids**.

Aphid

Ants

There are many different kinds of ants.

Ants live almost everywhere.

They live with other ants.

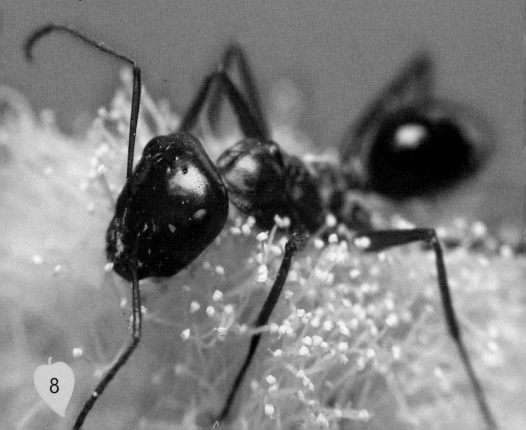

Ants eat other insects.

Ants also eat the **honeydew** that aphids make.

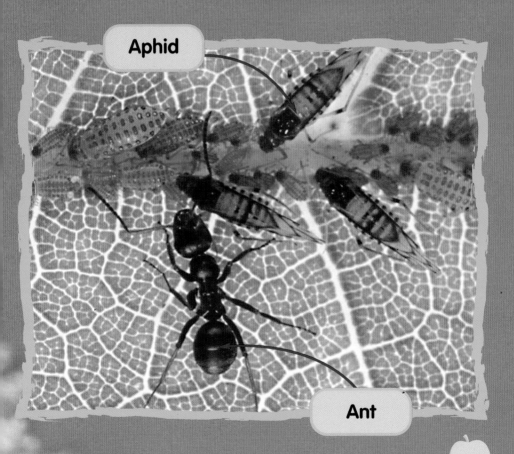

Aphid

Ant

Dragonflies

There are many different kinds of dragonflies.

They eat other flying insects.

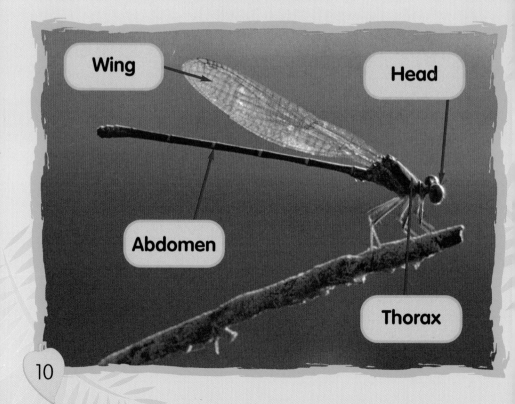

Wing

Head

Abdomen

Thorax

Dragonflies live near water.

The adults live on land and in the air.

The young live underwater.

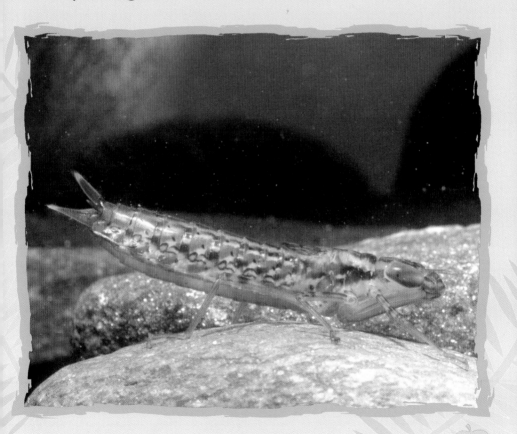

Butterflies

There are many different kinds of butterflies.

They feed on the **nectar** from flowers.

Antenna

Wings

Butterflies live in the air and on plants and flowers.

Head lice

Head lice live on clean hair.

They feed on human blood.

Head lice do not have wings.

They cannot fly.

They jump from head to head.

Abdomen

Leg

Antenna

Head

Thorax

15

Aphids

Aphids live on plants and trees.

They eat the **sap** in the leaves.

Aphids make honeydew.

Aphids

16

Ladybugs eat aphids.

Ant

Ants eat the honeydew.

17

Honeybees

Some honeybees live in hives.

Some live in trees.

They all live with other honeybees.

Hive

Honeybees feed on nectar from flowers.

They turn the nectar into honey.

Honeybee

Life cycles

All insects change as they get older.

Some insects go through two life cycle changes.

They change like this:

Eggs → Nymph → Adult

These bugs go through two big changes in their lives.

Other insects go through three life cycle changes.

They change like this:

| Eggs | → | Larva | → | Pupa | → | Adult |

These bugs go through three big changes in their lives.

Glossary

abdomen (AB-duh-muhn) the back part of an insect's body

antennae (an-TEN-nee) feelers on top of an insect's head

aphids (AY-fids) small insects that suck the juice from plants

honeydew (HUHN-ee-doo) a sweet liquid made by aphids

insects (IN-sekts) small animals with bodies that have three parts

nectar (NEK-tur) a sweet liquid found in flowers

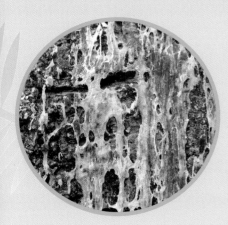

sap (SAP) a liquid in plants and trees

thorax (THOR-aks) the part of an insect's body between its head and abdomen

23

Index

Learn More

Rockwell, Anne. *Bugs Are Insects.* New York: HarperTrophy (2001).

Stewart, Melissa. *Insects.* Danbury, CT: Children's Press (2000).

www.ivyhall.district96.k12.il.us/4th/kkhp/1insects/bugmenu.html

www.urbanext.uiuc.edu/insects/01.html